A Natural You

Cheryl Smith

Presentation by *BookLeaf Publishing*

Web: www.bookleafpub.com

E-mail: info@bookleafpub.com

ISBN: 9789357441223

First edition 2023

ACKNOWLEDGEMENT

I want to firstly take time to thank my Mum for her love of reading and inspiring me to explore my creativity through language.

I also want to say a big thank you to my 'Queens' Christine, Polly, Jenny, Carol, Rosie, Jodie, Joanne and Kirstie. You are my biggest cheerleaders and have given me the confidence to believe in my writing.

Lastly to all of my English teachers who lit this passion up inside me and my love for the written word.

PREFACE

These poems are from my heart and love for the connection we have with nature. I feel at home outside, or at least looking outside. I feel strongly the energy we share with our planet, with Earth, Wind, Air and Fire. There are so many parallels to the life we lead and the environment around us. I hope when reading through this collection you gain a sense of the magnitude of this Universe and just how interlinked we all are.

A New Year

As the sun sets on another year,
it's much like waving off an old friend.
It may have seen laughter and a tear,
but on its merry way we must send.

It's time to look on the lessons,
and memories with fondness.
To let go and release tensions,
to wonder, what is beyond us?

So goodbye to the year behind
as it burns in the night sky,
with the fireworks, you'll find
your dreams up there, up high.

A Misty Morning

The trees stand tall in their half shed jackets.
Drops of morning dew, like crystals, clinging to
the branch.
Before their imminent drop to the mulchy
ground below.
The cars rumble past on their mundane
commute,
lights shining brightly, cutting the grey mist
that has descended upon our world.
The birds sing sweetly as they soar above me in
the sky,
looking for their morning fill.
Drizzly rain comes down around me, making the
landscape grainy,
as if I have stepped into an old film.
Houses are adorned with leftover Christmas
lights, resting from their
glow. Ready to take the night once more,
showing their majestic dance,
against the black night sky.
The grey, damp, misty morning holds a beauty
unbeknownst to most,
but as I walk cosy, amongst its chill, I see
nothing but pure magic.

The Sea Calms Me

The sea calms me,
Her waves crash and,
She hides secrets but,
To me she is a healer.

The sound she makes
Just soothes my core.
It connects me back,
To our Mother Earth.

The sea calms me,
I have no fear of her.
I respect her, as I know
She is part of me.

She ebbs and flows,
her tides rise and fall,
It reminds me of breathing
and to follow her lead.

The sea calms me,
An expanse so wonderous,
so majestic, all being.
The sea calms me.

Winter

As she curls up
ready to sleep,
she feels herself
falling like snowflakes.
Into a world
that is not her own.
Darkness.

Hide and Seek

Winter seeks as we hide.
We burrow deeply inwards
looking for the warmth around us,
but really we should look inside.
The warmth we seek does not
lie in log fires crackling,
fleecy blankets or hot cocoa.
But in the depths of our being.
Our hearts are a glow with
the warmest light in humanness;
our ability to love.

The Flower

Her seeds planted,
She nurtures herself.
Drinks water from
the heavens.
Takes in nutrients
from Mother Earth.
Her roots, stretch,
wind and clench down.
Down,
down
into the ground.
Planted.
Darkness.
She contemplates her
state. Then,
she shoots, bright, warm,
Sunlight. She breathes it in.
She gains strength,
She grows,
She rises from the roots.
She doesn't seek permission,
She blooms, bright and bold.
She stands tall,
Facing the sun.
The light becomes her.
The flower.

FREE

Enough
Take a step back,
Breathe
Close your eyes,
Escape
Feel your heart beat,
Strong
Stand up tall,
Proud
Don't be afraid,
Trust
Speak your truth,
Loud
Spread your wings,
Fly
Soar in the clouds,
High
Release everything,
FREE.

The Moon

Her phases hold power
That many men don't know,
She shines in the darkness,
Encourages us to let go.

She illuminates the sky
in her fullness, shines bright.
The phase of her newness,
She hides behind the light.

She controls our waters,
pulls on our tides.
She charges our crystals,
Rules our energies inside.

We follow her cycles,
through the full to the new.
We learn so much from her,
Those awakened are few.

So in the night darkness,
look up to the sky,
and whisper your dreams,
release your fears in a cry.

She'll listen to it all
and hold onto it tight.
So when you feel lonely,
she'll remind you of that night.

Her

She dances in the rain
With a smile on her face.
Her heart beats faster
When she sees the moon full.
Her skin bumps as her toes
Scrunch in the sand
And she breathes deep
As the sun bathes across her face.
This is her language
This is her soul
This is her
Free.

A New Beginning

A chance to start fresh,
Wipe the slate clean.
Shake off the dreary winter.

Step into Spring,
with a renewed hope.
Just like the buds in the trees.

Say goodbye to darkness,
as you emerge, strong,
ready to bloom and grow.

Him

Here he comes,
The one!
He gives me warmth,
like no other.
When I turn my face to him,
I glow and smile.
He illuminates me.
He makes my skin glitter golden.
I watch as he rises,
when most of the world sleeps.
He holds me , gives me strength
for the day ahead.
He lights not only me,
but all who he touches.
His power is incomprehensible.
He has a fire that if I'm not careful,
burns me.
But I know deep down within me,
he has never meant to harm.
He is the most breathtaking
thing from the moment he
wakes through to his last look
of the day.
He gives me life,
of course, He,
is the Sun.

Follow that Call

When the trees dance in the breeze,
and invite you into their waltz,
go dance with them.
Twirl, hop, walk with arms outstretched.
Follow that call.

When the river glitters in the beams of the sun,
and invites you into it's depths,
go bathe with it.
Wade, paddle, splash with a smile on face.
Follow that call.

When the green fields blades run wild,
and they invite you into the race,
go run with them.
Run fast, skip, roll in their softness.
Follow that call.

When our Mother Nature sings her song,
and she invites you into the chorus,
go sing with her.
Whistle, laugh, breathe into her air.
Follow that call.

Fire

She felt the fire
Burning inside her.
Hot as the sun,
just like before.
This was different,
she wasn't burning down
but glowing upwards,
just as the sun's rays.
The embers flared
from inside her heart,
captured her ambition
and drive for success.
She was rising through
the flames like a Phoenix.
She was on fire,
burning bright,
her whole being alight.
The wonder and passion,
from being her true self.

A Summer Haiku

The sunbeams shine bright.
Smiles on peoples faces, joy.
Summer is happy.

The Summer Sky

Into the bright blue sky
I stare.
Longing, wishing, to be
Up there.
Free

AUTUMN

All the wonderous colours fill the world,
Until the winter freezes them away.
The trees blow in the autumn winds
Uniting the leaves in piles on the ground.
Many gain joy in this season,
Noting how change can bring beauty.

The Joy of Leaves

The trees blow to and fro in the
blustery winds of Autumn.
The leaves hold on tight not wanting
to leave, but they know the fall will come.
They float, spin, dive and dance down,
settling in groups together.
People smile and collect the leaves,
they throw them up as light as feathers.
It brings joy and a sense of childhood fun,
as people play and frolic this season.
Although it lasts a mere 12 weeks,
when we are in it, autumn never feels done.

An Autumn Haiku

19

The autumn colours
Pop, in the morning sunlight
The world is waking.

The Tree

As the trees bow and bend,
their leaves fly away.
No one sees their sadness.
Their tears are silent,
but their heart wrenching
loneliness can be seen in
their bareness.

It's OK

Just like autumn
It's ok for us to fall,
It's ok for us to change.
When we shed and let go
We experience what it's
Like to grow.

I Am You

The blood runs through my veins,
As sure as the rivers run from source to sea.
I am you.

My lungs rise and fall with every breath,
As the ocean ebbs and flows to the shore.
I am you.

My eyes open wide each morning,
In time with the sun rising for a new day.
I am you.

They close to the darkness of the night,
Parallel to the setting sun and moon glow.
I am you.

My bones, the structure hold me strong and tall,
In reflection to your oldest barks in the deepest
forests.
I am you.

My heart beats loudly reminding me of life
itself,
To the drum of Mother Nature and her song.
I am you.

My brain holds the intellect of this vessel,
As it shares with everything I see.
I am you.

Everything that Mother Nature holds,
Is within me because,
I am you.

www.ingramcontent.com/pod-product-compliance
Lightning Source LLC
La Vergne TN
LVHW021346200726
843509LV00014B/2696